**SCHOLASTIC**

# News

**Nonfiction Readers®**

## Our Earth
# Saving Energy

## by Peggy Hock

Children's Press®
An Imprint of Scholastic Inc.
New York  Toronto  London  Auckland  Sydney
Mexico City  New Delhi  Hong Kong
Danbury, Connecticut

These content vocabulary word builders are for grades 1–2.

Content Adviser: Zoe Chafe, Research Associate, Worldwatch Institute, Washington, DC

Reading Consultant: Cecilia Minden-Cupp, PhD, Early Literacy Consultant and Author, Chapel Hill, North Carolina

Book Design: Simonsays Design!
Book Production: The Design Lab

Library of Congress Cataloging-in-Publication Data
Hock, Peggy, 1948–
Saving energy / By Peggy Hock.
  p. cm.—(Scholastic news nonfiction readers)
Includes bibliographical references and index.
ISBN-13: 978-0-531-13835-9 (lib. bdg.) 978-0-531-20435-1 (pbk.)
ISBN-10: 0-531-13835-6 (lib. bdg.) 0-531-20435-9 (pbk.)
1. Energy conservation—Juvenile literature. I. Title. II. Series.
TJ163.35.H63 2008
333.79—dc22                          2007051898

# CONTENTS

# WORD HUNT

Look for these words as you read. They will be in **bold**.

**air pollution**
(ayr puh-**loo**-shuhn)

**gasoline**
(gas-uh-**leen**)

**oil**
(oyl)

**coal**
(kohl)

**electrical outlet**
(ih-**lek**-trih-kuhl
**out**-let)

**power plant**
(**pow**-uhr plant)

**recycle**
(ree-**sye**-kuhl)

5

# Using Energy

Look around. Can you see where energy is being used?

Energy is used to heat buildings and run cars.

Energy is also used by everything that plugs into an **electrical outlet**.

**electrical outlet**

**How many different ways do you use energy each day?**

People use **oil** and **coal** to get much of the energy they need.

Oil is used to make **gasoline** for cars.

Coal and natural gas are burned in **power plants**.

gasoline

oil

coal

**Many power plants burn coal to make electricity.**

Burning coal, oil, and other things creates **air pollution**.

That is one reason to use less energy.

Someday, people may not be able to find enough oil and coal to use.

That is another good reason to save energy!

What can you do to save energy?

Big cities like Los Angeles have air pollution. Air pollution is not healthy for people.

Saving gas is one way to save energy.

Taking fewer car trips saves gas.

Could you ride your bike or walk to school?

That would save gas.

Taking the bus saves gas, too.

A bus can hold many kids. Getting all these kids to school in cars would use a lot more gas.

How else can you save energy?

You can save energy by using less electricity.

Turn off the lights when you leave a room.

Make sure to turn off computers and TVs when you are not using them.

The funny-looking lightbulb on the right helps people save energy. It uses much less energy than the regular lightbulb.

Another way to save energy is to use less plastic.

Making plastic and other things in factories uses a lot of energy.

Use plastic packages more than once, if you can.

And remember to **recycle**. It takes less energy to make things from recycled plastic than from new plastic.

**Recycling plastic, paper, and metal helps save energy.**

Can you think of other ways to save energy at school and at home?

Talk to an adult and share your ideas.

Then make your own energy-saving plan!

You can save energy by turning off the TV when you are done watching it.

# Five Easy Ways to Save Energy

**1**

Put on a sweater instead of turning up the heat in winter.

**2**

Cut down on car trips. Bike, carpool, or take a bus when you can.

**5**

Open a window and use a fan instead of an air conditioner in the summer.

**4**

Recycle and buy recycled products.

**3**

Turn off the lights when you leave a room.

# YOUR NEW WORDS

**air pollution** (ayr puh-**loo**-shuhn) harmful materials that make the air dirty and unhealthy to breathe

**coal** (kohl) a hard, black rock that is burned to produce electricity

**electrical outlet** (ih-**lek**-trih-kuhl **out**-let) an opening in a wall that leads to a source of electricity

**gasoline** (gas-uh-**leen**) liquid fuel that is made from oil found underground

**oil** (oyl) a thick liquid found underground that is used to make gasoline and other products

**power plants** (**pow**-uhr plants) places where fuel is burned to make electricity

**recycle** (ree-**sye**-kuhl) to make old plastic, paper, glass, and metal into new objects

# WHERE DOES ENERGY COME FROM?

Coal or oil (or natural gas, not shown)

Moving water

Sunshine

Wind

# INDEX

## FIND OUT MORE

**Book:**

Green, Jen. *Why Should I Save Energy?* Hauppauge, NY: Barron's Educational Series, Inc., 2005.

**Website:**

Energy Quest
*http://www.energyquest.ca.gov*

## MEET THE AUTHOR

Peggy Hock lives near San Francisco, California. She likes to go backpacking with her husband and two grown children. She uses compact fluorescent lightbulbs in her lamps.